3rd Edition
Ventures
LITERACY WORKBOOK
BASIC

Gretchen Bitterlin ▪ **Dennis Johnson** ▪ **Donna Price** ▪ **Sylvia Ramirez**

K. Lynn Savage (Series Editor)

with Linda Mrowicki

CAMBRIDGE
UNIVERSITY PRESS

CAMBRIDGE
UNIVERSITY PRESS

University Printing House, Cambridge CB2 8BS, United Kingdom

One Liberty Plaza, 20th Floor, New York, NY 10006, USA

477 Williamstown Road, Port Melbourne, VIC 3207, Australia

314–321, 3rd Floor, Plot 3, Splendor Forum, Jasola District Centre, New Delhi – 110025, India

103 Penang Road, #05-06/07, Visioncrest Commercial, Singapore 238467

Cambridge University Press is part of the University of Cambridge.

It furthers the University's mission by disseminating knowledge in the pursuit of education, learning and research at the highest international levels of excellence.

www.cambridge.org
Information on this title: www.cambridge.org/9781108449663

First published 2008
Second edition 2014

20 19 18 17 16 15 14 13 12 11 10 9 8 7 6

Printed in Mexico by Litográfica Ingramex, S.A. de C.V.

A catalogue record for this publication is available from the British Library

ISBN 978-1-108-44953-3 Student's Book
ISBN 978-1-108-44998-4 Workbook
ISBN 978-1-108-44932-8 Online Workbook
ISBN 978-1-108-57321-4 Teacher's Edition
ISBN 978-1-108-44919-9 Class Audio CDs
ISBN 978-1-108-45027-0 Presentation Plus

Additional resources for this publication at www.cambridge.org/ventures

CONTENTS

INTRODUCTION

What is the *Ventures Literacy Workbook*?

The ***Ventures Literacy Workbook*** is designed to accompany the ***Ventures Basic Student's Book***. This workbook provides reading and writing readiness activities targeted specifically to literacy learners. It takes into account the six main types of students in need of literacy instruction[1]:

1. **preliterate learners:** whose first language either has no writing system or has a writing system that is relatively recent and/or not commonly used in daily life. The language of the Hmong of Southeast Asia is an example.

2. **nonliterate learners:** whose first language has a writing system that is used in daily life but who have not been schooled in that writing system. Examples include those whose schooling was disrupted because of regional unrest and those from subgroups forbidden by government policy from being schooled.

3. **semiliterate learners:** whose first language has a writing system that is used in daily life but whose schooling was either incomplete or unsuccessful. Adult students who left school before completing primary grades are examples.

4. **nonalphabet literate learners:** whose first language has a writing system that represents ideas rather than sounds. Chinese is an example.

5. **non-Roman alphabet literate learners:** whose first language uses a writing system that has symbols for sounds, but the symbols are not Roman letters. Two of the three Japanese scripts (hiragana and katakana), Russian, and Arabic are examples.

6. **Roman alphabet literate learners:** whose first language writing system uses the Roman alphabet but associates certain letters with different sounds than those used in English. Their writing systems may not use all the letters in the English alphabet or may include other letters not used in the English alphabet. French, Italian, and Spanish are examples.

How is the *Ventures Literacy Workbook* different from the *Ventures Basic Workbook*?

There are two workbooks to accompany the *Ventures Basic Student's Book*. The two workbooks can be used by different groups of students within the same classroom, providing meaningful, appropriate activities for a range of levels in a multilevel teaching situation.

The ***Ventures Basic Workbook*** provides written activities and audio to reinforce the aural/oral language taught in the Student's Book. It is targeted to students who already possess reading and writing skills and provides reinforcement activities at the same level as the lessons in the Student's Book. The vocabulary and structures in each lesson come from the corresponding lesson in the Student's Book. The ***Ventures Basic Workbook*** is designed for independent use outside of class, although it can also be used for additional in-class practice.

The ***Ventures Literacy Workbook***, in contrast, provides reading, writing, and listening readiness activities targeted to literacy students who, for reasons listed above, need to learn and practice the Roman alphabet and focus on learning to read and write individual words and phrases. The letters practiced in each lesson, and the words used to exemplify these letters, are taken from the corresponding lesson in the Student's Book. The ***Ventures Literacy Workbook*** is designed for in-class use so that literacy students can practice writing with the guidance of teachers and/or classmates with developed literacy skills.

Both workbooks reinforce the themes and language presented in the Student's Book and practiced in class.

The differences between the ***Ventures Literacy Workbook*** and the ***Ventures Basic Workbook*** are outlined in the chart on page v.

---

[1] ERIC Brief "Reading and Adult English Language Learners: The Role of the First Language" (Center for Applied Linguistics)

Differences between the *Literacy Workbook* and the *Basic Workbook*

Literacy Workbook	Basic Workbook
Target learners: - learners whose first language has no traditional writing system (preliterate) - learners not literate or not fully literate in their first language writing system (nonliterate or semiliterate) - learners literate in a first language that uses a non-Roman alphabet or a nonalphabetic writing system (non-Roman alphabet literate or nonalphabet literate) - learners literate in a first language that associates different sounds than English does for some letters in the Roman alphabet or has more or fewer letters in its alphabet (Roman alphabet literate)	**Target learners:** - true beginners literate in a first language that has a writing system based on the Roman alphabet
Goal: - to develop reading and writing readiness skills	**Goal:** - to reinforce through written activities the language taught in the Student's Book
Assumptions: - students need instruction in the mechanical skills involved in forming letters - students need development in the concept that print represents spoken language - students need instruction in English writing conventions (left to right, on the line)	**Assumptions:** - students are able to recognize and form capital and lowercase letters in the Roman alphabet - students are able to relate sounds to print - students are able to follow English writing conventions (left to right, on the line)
Tasks: - recognize differences between letters - trace and copy letters following stroke order - relate capital letters to lowercase letters - read and copy words and phrases	**Tasks:** - complete words and phrases in response to written cues - apply higher-order thinking skills to written tasks - read and interpret short passages and documents - complete real-life writing tasks
Setting: - designed for in-class use with teacher and/or peer guidance - no answer key	**Setting:** - designed for independent study outside of class - contains answer key

How is the *Ventures Literacy Workbook* structured?

In order to address the needs of a variety of literacy learners, the Literacy Workbook has a unique structure. There are two pages for each lesson in the Student's Book, at two different levels of literacy.

☑ ■ The left-hand page, the first for each lesson, is designed for students who need to focus on the individual letters of the Roman alphabet, in both uppercase and lowercase. These are most often students who are preliterate, nonliterate, or semiliterate in their own languages.

■ ☑ The right-hand page, the second for each lesson, is designed for students who need to practice reading, copying, and writing individual words and phrases. These are most often students who are literate in their own language but whose writing system is nonalphabetic or uses a non-Roman alphabet.

Students whose first language writing system uses the Roman alphabet differently than it is used in English can move back and forth between the two pages. For these students, certain letters may represent different sounds than they do in their writing system, and the English alphabet may contain more or fewer letters. When they encounter a letter not in their writing system, they can start with the left-hand page. When the letters are ones they are familiar with, they may do the right-hand page only.

Students already literate in the Roman alphabet may be ready to complete pages in the Basic Workbook in addition to the Literacy Workbook.

What is the relationship between the left-hand page and the right-hand page?

Depending on their level and situation, students can complete just the left-hand page, just the right-hand page, or both pages in the Literacy Workbook. The key letters and words presented on the left-hand page appear again in a slightly different form on the right-hand page, so that the first page leads into the second. This creates a progression within the lesson for students who opt to complete both pages.

For example, in Unit 1, Lesson A, the pre-, semi-, and nonliterate students learn the block capital letters *L*, *T*, and *F*. At the end of the page, students trace those letters in the words *FIRST* and *LAST*.

The right-hand page begins with the words *FIRST*, *LAST*, and *NAME* in both block capital letters and lowercase letters. Students who complete the left-hand side with confidence will be able to move to the right-hand side. Students who begin with the right-hand side but feel less confident or need some remediation (such as reviewing stroke order) can move to the left-hand side and then return to the right-hand side.

The chart on page vii highlights the relationship between the two pages.

What is the rationale behind the order in which letters are presented?

The *Ventures Literacy Workbook* presents the letters not in alphabetical order, but in a carefully designed sequence. This sequence was determined according to three criteria: (1) the context in the Student's Book, (2) the frequency of the letter's occurrence in English, and (3) the type of strokes used to form the letter (e.g., horizontal and vertical as in *E* and *L*, diagonal as in *K*, circular as in *O* and *e*, taller strokes as in *b* and *h*, and strokes that go below the line, as in *g* and *y*).

Extra practice pages for additional work in forming letters appear in the back of the Literacy Workbook, presented in the same order as in the lessons. Three low-frequency letters – *Xx*, *Zz*, and *Qq* – are covered in the Extra practice section only.

How do I use the *Literacy Workbook*?

Use the *Ventures Literacy Workbook* to provide your literacy students with level-appropriate writing activities at any point during a *Ventures* lesson. Pages in the Literacy Workbook can be assigned whenever the majority of the class is engaged in an activity that involves reading and writing at a level that is beyond your literacy students' skills.

Assign either the left-hand page or the right-hand page, depending on each student's literacy level and background or encourage particular students to try both pages. Be sure to model writing the letters and watch students closely as they trace and copy letters for the first time to make sure they follow correct stroke order and move from left to right across the page.

Pair your literacy students with other students in the class who have more advanced literacy skills. This promotes community in the classroom and frees you to work with more groups individually.

The *Ventures Literacy Workbook* focuses on the recognition and formation of letters in meaningful contexts. Once learners have developed these skills, you may want to introduce phonics – the connection between letter patterns and the sounds they represent. This is usually done with word families and begins with initial sounds. For example, the word *NAME*, presented in the first lesson, belongs to the word family *–AME*. By the end of Unit 1, learners have learned the letters *N*, *L*, *T*, *F*, *C*, and *G*. All of these can be added to *–AME* to form new words. With flash cards for these letters and a flash card for the word family *–AME*, you can help students begin to see and use phonics to decode words.

There is no answer key for the *Ventures Literacy Workbook*. All answers are evident on the page. As students complete each page, be sure to check and correct their work.

Additional worksheets for each letter and blank writing grids can be printed from the Ventures online resources (www.cambridge.org/ventures/resources/) for further practice, either in the classroom or as homework.

Relationship between the left-hand and right-hand pages

☑ ■ Left-hand page	■ ☑ Right-hand page
Goal: By the end of the workbook, students will be able to: ■ form letters ■ read and copy words and phrases	**Goal:** By the end of the workbook, students will be able to: ■ read and copy sentences
Target learners: ■ learners not fully literate in their first language (preliterate, nonliterate, and semiliterate students)	**Target learners:** ■ learners literate in their first language (Roman alphabet literate, non-Roman alphabet literate, and nonalphabet literate students)
Focus: Individual letters ■ Units 1–2: block capitals ■ Units 3–5: lowercase letters ■ Units 5–10: decreased font size, relation between capital and lowercase letters	**Focus:** Words, phrases, and sentences ■ Units 1–4: words and phrases ■ Units 5–6: phrases and sentences ■ Units 7–10: questions and answers
Sequence of activities: ■ Read. *Purpose:* to provide a focus ■ Circle the same. *Purpose:* to distinguish shapes before writing ■ Read. Trace. Copy. *Purpose:* to develop production skills	**Sequence of activities:** ■ Read. Copy. *Purpose:* to provide a focus ■ Read. Trace. Circle the same. *Purpose:* to develop recognition skills ■ Read. Trace. Copy. *Purpose:* to develop production skills

TRACE. COPY.

0   0

1   1

2   2   2   2

3   3   3   3

4   4   4   4

COUNT. TRACE. COPY.

1   1

4   4

7   7

Listen. Read.

1   4   7   9

◀)) Track 2

Count. Trace. Copy.

1

4

7

9

TRACE. COPY.

5   1   5   5   5

6   6

7   7   7   7

8   8   8   8

9   0   9   9

COUNT. TRACE. COPY.

   0   0

   3   3

   8   8

Listen. Read.

◀)) Track 3

0   3   8   5   6

Count. Trace. Copy.

0   0 _____

3   3 _____

8   8 _____

5   5 _____

6   6 _____

Lesson A Listening

CIRCLE THE SAME. L T (L) F T (L)

L	T	L	F	T	L
T	F	T	T	L	F
F	F	T	F	L	T

READ. TRACE. COPY.

L   L   L   L

T   T   T   T

F   F   F   F

TRACE. READ.

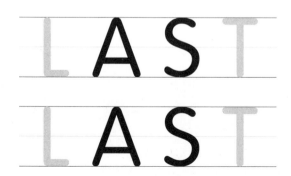

FIRST   LAST

FIRST   LAST

Listen. Trace.

FIRST   first

LAST   last

NAME   name

Read. Trace. Circle the same.   first (first) fist (first) fist

first   first   fist   first   fist

last   last   lass   lass   last

name   man   name   name   man

Read. Trace. Copy.

first   first

last   last

name   name

Read. Copy.

first name

last name

CIRCLE THE SAME. O Ⓞ Ⓞ C C G

O	O	O	C	C	G
C	G	C	O	C	C
U	O	U	C	U	U

READ. TRACE. COPY.

O O

C C

U U

TRACE. READ.

COUNTRY CHINA

COUNTRY CHINA

Lesson B Countries

Trace. Read.

COUNTRY   country

CHINA   China

UNITED STATES   United States

Read. Trace. Circle the same.   country count count (country)

country   count   count   country

China   China   China   Chain

Read. Trace. Copy.

the   the

United   United

States   States

Read. Copy.

the United States

CIRCLE THE SAME. I Ⓘ Ⓘ I E E H

I I I E E H

H E H I H H

E H I E H E

READ. TRACE. COPY.

I I I I I

H I H H

E I I F F E

TRACE. READ.

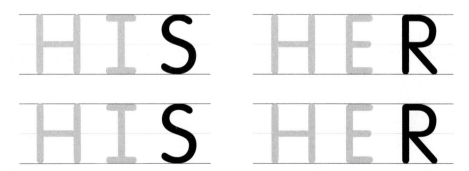

HIS HER

HIS HER

Lesson C What's your name?

Trace. Read.

HIS his

HER her

Read. Trace. Circle the same.   his is (his) (his) (his) is

his   is   his   his   his   is

her   her   her   her   here   here

Read. Trace. Copy.

Registration Form

First name: Hui

his first name

_____ first name

Registration Form

Last name: Li

her last name

_____ last name

CIRCLE THE SAME. J L Ⓙ T L Ⓙ

J L J T L J

V V W N V W

G C G G C O

READ. TRACE. COPY.

J J J J

V V V V

G C G G

TRACE. READ.

JUNE NOV. AUG.

JUNE NOV. AUG.

Lesson D Reading

Read. Trace. Copy.

January	January
February	February
March	March
April	April
May	May
June	June
July	July
August	August
September	September
October	October
November	November
December	December

READ.

VALLEY ADULT SCHOOL
LAST NAME: LEE
AREA CODE: 212
PHONE NUMBER: 555-7834

TRACE. READ.

VALLEY ADULT SCHOOL
LAST NAME: LEE
AREA CODE: 212
PHONE NUMBER: 555-7834

Lesson E Writing

Trace. Read.

AREA CODE   area code

PHONE NUMBER   phone number

Read. Trace. Write.

Jeff	Cho
First name	Last name
708	555-8421
Area code	Phone number

First name: Jeff

Last name: _____

Area code: _____

Phone number: _____

READ.

NAME: JOE LIU
AREA CODE: 209
PHONE NUMBER: 555-7416

TRACE.

NAME

JOE LIU

AREA CODE

209

PHONE NUMBER

555-7416

Read. Trace. Write.

STUDENT ID

First name _____ Lee

Last name _____ Loc

Area code _____ 312

Phone number _____ 555-9846

STUDENT ID

First name _____ Lee

_____ Loc

_____ 312

_____ 555-9846

Lesson A Listening

CIRCLE THE SAME. A A N N A A

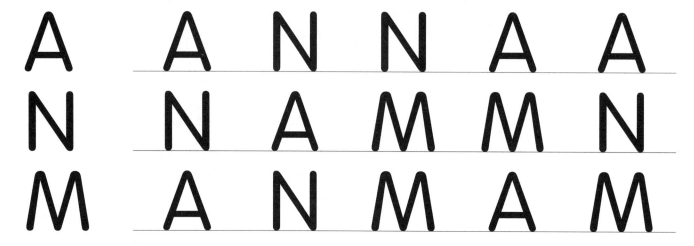

A	A	N	N	A	A
N	N	A	M	M	N
M	A	N	M	A	M

READ. TRACE. COPY.

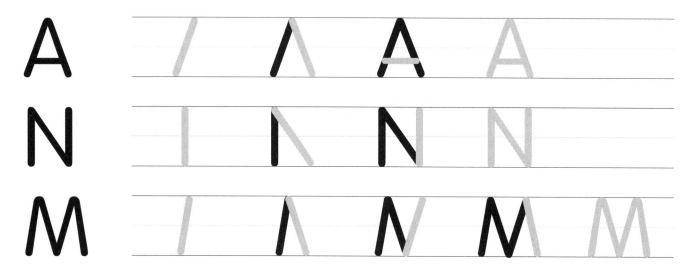

A

N

M

TRACE. READ.

CHAIR NAME

CHAIR NAME

■ ✓

Listen. Trace.

CHAIR   chair

PENCIL   pencil

NAME   name

◀)) Track 5

Read. Trace. Circle the same.   chair (chair) char (chair) char

chair   chair   char   chair   char

pencil   pen   pencil   pencil   pen

name   mane   name   name   mane

Read. Trace. Copy.

chair   chair

pencil   pencil

name   name

Read. Copy.

a pencil

a name

CIRCLE THE SAME.   S   (S)   Z   (S)   8   (S)

S	S	Z	S	8	S
P	P	B	P	P	R
R	B	R	R	P	R

READ. TRACE. COPY.

S   S

P   P   P

R   P   P   R

TRACE. READ.

STAPLER   RULER

STAPLER   RULER

Lesson B Classroom objects

Trace. Read.

STAPLER   stapler

RULER   ruler

ERASER   eraser

Read. Trace. Circle the same. stapler (stapler) staple (stapler)

stapler   stapler   staple   stapler

ruler   ruler   ruler   rule

eraser   erase   eraser   eraser

Read. Trace. Copy.

stapler   stapler

ruler   ruler

Read. Copy.

a stapler

a ruler

CIRCLE THE SAME. D D D B P D

D   D   D   B   P   D

B   D   P   B   P   B

READ. TRACE. COPY.

D   I   D   D

B   I   P   B   B

TRACE. READ.

DESK   BOOK

DESK   BOOK

Lesson C Where's my pencil?

Trace. Read.

IN   in   DESK   desk

ON   on   BOOK   book

UNDER   under

Read. Trace. Circle the same.   on   on   on   on   son

on   on   on   on   son

in   in   tin   in   in

under   under   under   untie   under

desk   desk   rest   desk   desk

book   book   book   hook   book

Read. Trace. Copy.

on the desk   on the desk

in the book   in the book

under the desk   under the desk

CIRCLE THE SAME.   K Ⓚ R B R Ⓚ

K   K   R   B   R   K

Y   X   Y   V   V   X

W   M   M   W   W   W

READ. TRACE. COPY.

K   K   K   K   K

Y   Y   Y   Y

W   W   W   W   W

TRACE. READ.

WEEK   DAY

WEEK   DAY

Lesson D Reading

Trace. Read.

WEEK   week

DAY   day

Read. Trace. Copy.

week   week

day   day

Sunday   Sunday

Monday   Monday

Tuesday   Tuesday

Wednesday   Wednesday

Thursday   Thursday

Friday   Friday

Saturday   Saturday

READ. CIRCLE THE SAME. PEN   PAN (PEN)

PEN   PAN   PEN
BOOK LOOK BOOK

READ. TRACE.

PEN   PEN   PEN
BOOK BOOK BOOK

TRACE. READ.

A PEN

A BOOK

Lesson E Writing

Read. Trace.

School Supplies

 an eraser

 a book

 a pen

 a pencil

Write.

_an_   _eraser_

READ.

SOUTH SIDE ADULT SCHOOL

CLASS: TUESDAY

THURSDAY

YOU NEED: PAPER

A PENCIL

TRACE. READ.

TUESDAY

THURSDAY

PAPER

PENCIL

Lesson F Another view

Read. Trace.

Kennedy Adult School English Class

Monday Tuesday Thursday Friday

You need

 ☑ a book

 ☑ a pen

 ☑ a pencil

 ☑ paper

Write the days.

Monday _____ _____ _____

What do students need?

a   book

___   _____

___   _____

_____

Lesson A Listening

CIRCLE THE SAME. a o ⓐ ⓐ e ⓐ

a   o   a   a   e   a

e   e   c   e   o   e

r   r   n   r   n   r

READ. TRACE. WRITE.

a   o   a   a

e   e   e   e

r   r   r   r

TRACE. READ.

father   mother

father   mother

Listen. Trace.

Track 6

FATHER   father

MOTHER   mother

GRAND   grand

Read. Trace. Circle the same.   father   farther   (father)   (father)

father   farther   father   father

mother   mother   other   mother

grand   gland   grand   grand

Read. Trace. Copy.

father   father _____

mother   mother _____

grand   grand _____

Read. Copy.

grandfather _____

grandmother _____

CIRCLE THE SAME. i (i) l t (i) l

i   i   l   t   i   l

c   o   e   e   c   c

u   n   u   v   v   u

READ. TRACE. COPY.

i   i   i   i

c   c

u   u   u   u

TRACE. READ.

wife   uncle

wife   uncle

Lesson B Family members

Trace. Read.

WIFE   wife

UNCLE   uncle

AUNT   aunt

Read. Trace. Circle the same. wife life (wife) (wife) life

wife   life   wife   wife   life

uncle   uncle   uncle   unclear   uncle

aunt   aunt   aunt   ant   aunt

Read. Trace. Copy.

wife   wife

uncle   uncle

aunt   aunt

Read. Copy.

a wife

an uncle

CIRCLE THE SAME.   d   b   d   p   d   b

d   b   d   p   d   b

b   b   d   h   d   d

h   h   b   n   h   n

READ. TRACE. COPY.

d   o   d   d

b | b   b

h | h   h

TRACE. READ.

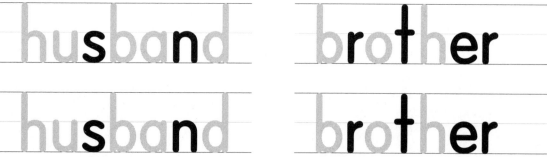

husband   brother

husband   brother

Lesson C Do you have a sister?

Trace. Read.

HUSBAND   husband

DAUGHTER   daughter

BROTHER   brother

Read. Trace. Circle the same. husband   his band   (husband)

husband   his band   husband

daughter   daughter   laughter

brother   bother   brother

Read. Trace. Copy.

husband   husband

daughter   daughter

brother   brother

Read. Copy.

a husband   _____

a brother   _____

READ. CIRCLE THE SAME. birth (birth) berth (birth)

birth   birth   berth   birth

day   bay   bay   day

READ. TRACE.

birth   birth   birth   birth

day   day   day   day

TRACE. READ.

birthday   birthday

Lesson D Reading

Trace. Read.

BIRTHDAY   birthday

GIRL   girl

BOY   boy

Read. Trace. Circle the same.   birthday   day   day   (birthday)

birthday   day   day   birthday

girl   grill   grill   girl

boy   boy   bay   boy

Read. Trace. Copy.

birthday   birthday

girl   girl

boy   boy

Read. Copy.

girl and boy

TRACE. READ.

husband

wife

READ. TRACE.

husband   husband

wife   wife

TRACE. READ.

husband and wife

Trace. Copy.

1. husband

2. wife

3. brother

4. sister

Read. Copy.

brother and sister

husband and wife

TRACE.

1. **mot**her

2. **f**a**t**her

3. dau**g**t**er

TRACE. READ.

mother and **f**a**t**her

Trace. Copy.

1. grandmother

2. grandfather

3. mother

4. father

5. daughter

Read. Copy.

grandmother and grandfather

CIRCLE THE SAME.

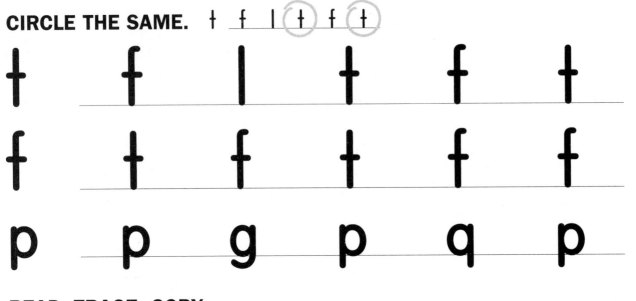

t   f   l   t   f   t

f   t   f   t   f   f

p   p   g   p   q   p

READ. TRACE. COPY.

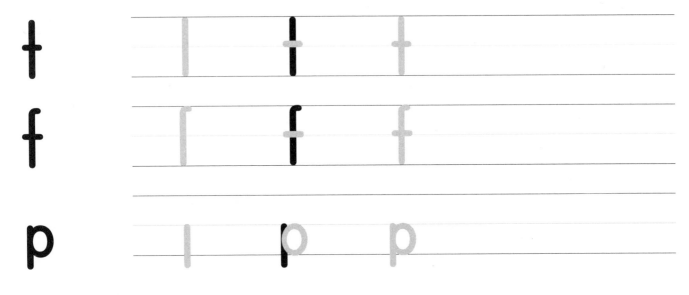

t

f

p

TRACE. READ.

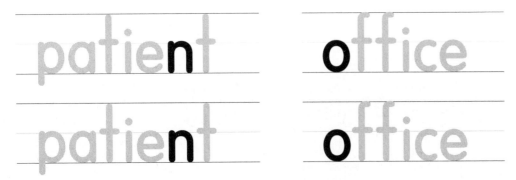

patient   office

patient   office

Listen. Trace.

🔊 Track 7

PATIENT   patient

OFFICE   office

DOCTOR   doctor

Read. Trace. Circle the same.   patient (patient) (patient) patent

patient   patient   patient   patent

office   office   offer   office

doctor   dock   doctor   doctor

Read. Trace. Copy.

patient   patient

office   office

doctor   doctor

Read. Copy.

patient   _____

office   _____

CIRCLE THE SAME.   o   o   c   o   c   o

o   o   c   o   c   o

n   m   n   n   m   n

m   m   m   n   n   m

READ. TRACE. COPY.

o   o

n   l   n   n

m   l   n   n   m

TRACE. READ.

s tomach   hand

s tomach   hand

Lesson B Parts of the body

Trace. Read.

STOMACH   stomach

HAND   hand

FOOT   foot

ARM   arm

Read. Trace. Circle the same.   stomach   storm   (stomach)   storm

stomach	storm	stomach	storm
hand	head	hand	hand
foot	foot	fool	foot
arm	arm	arm	arms

Read. Trace. Copy.

stomach   stomach

Read. Copy.

my stomach

CIRCLE THE SAME. s z s z s z

S Z S Z S Z

l i l t l l

g y j g g y

READ. TRACE. WRITE.

s   s

l   l

g   o g g

TRACE. READ.

legs   eyes

legs   eyes

Lesson C My feet hurt.

Trace. Read.

LEGS   legs

EYES   eyes

HANDS   hands

Read. Trace. Circle the same. legs (legs) (legs) (legs) leg

legs legs   legs   legs   leg

eyes eyes   eyes   eyes   eyes

hands hands   hand   hands   hands

Read. Trace. Copy.

legs legs

eyes eyes

hands hands

Read. Copy.

2 legs _____

2 eyes _____

READ. CIRCLE THE SAME. cold old (cold)

cold   old cold old

sore   sole sore sore

throat   oat throat oat

READ. TRACE. COPY.

cold   cold

sore   sore

throat   throat

TRACE. READ.

a cold

a sore throat

Lesson D Reading

Trace. Read.

SORE THROAT   sore throat

COLD   cold

HEADACHE   headache

Read. Trace. Copy.

a sore throat

a sore throat

a cold

a cold

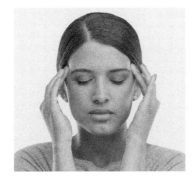

a headache

a headache

READ. CIRCLE THE SAME.   tooth (tooth) teeth

tooth	tooth	teeth
head	head	bead
ache	acne	ache

READ. TRACE. COPY.

tooth	tooth
head	head
ache	ache

TRACE. READ.

a toothache

a headache

Lesson E Writing

Read. Trace. Write.

DOCTOR'S OFFICE

Patient	Reason for visit
Carrie	sore throat
Linda	stomachache
Bud	headache
Ali	cold
Rae	toothache

Carrie _sore throat_____

Linda _____

Bud _____

Ali _____

Rae _____

READ.

MEDICINE FOR

- ☑ legs
- ☑ hands
- ☑ eyes
- ☑ stomach

TRACE. READ. COPY.

legs

hands

eyes

stomach

Lesson F Another view

Read. Trace.

MEDICINE FOR

eyes

legs

hands

stomach

Write.

eyes

_____

_____   _____

UNIT 5 AROUND TOWN

Lesson A Listening

CIRCLE THE SAME. k h ⓚ ⓚ h ⓚ

k	h	k	k	h	k
w	v	w	w	v	w
y	v	y	y	v	y

READ. TRACE. COPY.

k   k   k   k

w   v   v   w   w

y   y   y

TRACE. READ.

bank   town   library

bank   town   library

Listen. Trace.

Track 8

BANK   bank

TOWN   town

LIBRARY   library

Read. Trace. Circle the same. bank back (bank) back

bank   back   bank   back

town   town   town   down

library   literary   library   library

Read. Trace. Copy.

bank   bank

town   town

library   library

Read. Copy.

the bank

the town

CIRCLE THE SAME. v   v   w   u   v   v

v   v   w   u   v   v

j   j   g   j   g   j

READ. TRACE. COPY.

v   \   v   v

j   j   j

TRACE. READ. COPY.

movie

jacket

Lesson B Places around town

Trace. Read.

MOVIE   movie

THEATER   theater

JACKET   jacket

Read. Trace. Circle the same.   movie   (movie)   move   (movie)

movie   movie   move   movie

theater   theater   theater   heater

jacket   jackpot   jacket   jacket

Read. Trace. Copy.

movie   movie

theater   theater

jacket   jacket

Read. Copy.

movie theater

TRACE. READ.

across from

next to

READ. TRACE. CIRCLE THE SAME.   across   cross   (across)

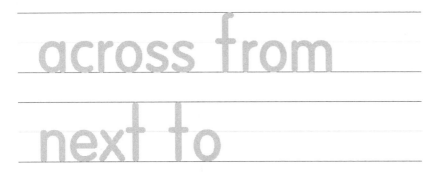

across	cross	across
from	from	form
next	next	nest
to	too	to

TRACE. READ. COPY.

across from

next to

Lesson C The school is on Main Street.

Trace. Read.

next to   across from

on   between

Read. Circle.

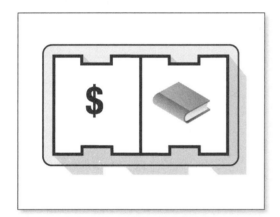

Where's the bank?

(Next to the library.)

Next to the post office.

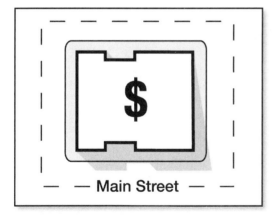

— Main Street —

Where's the bank?

On Fifth Street.

On Main Street.

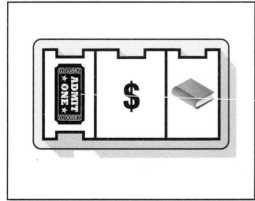

Where's the bank?

Across from the library.

Between the library
and the movie theater.

TRACE. READ.

BUS bus   CAR car

BY by

READ. TRACE. CIRCLE THE SAME.   bus (bus) bun (bus)

bus   bus bun bus

car   ear ear car

by   by bye bye

TRACE. READ. COPY.

by bus

by car

Lesson D Reading

Trace. Read. Circle the correct words.

(by bus)   by bus   by train

by car   by train   by car

Write.

by train

TRACE. READ.

ON   on

STREET street

READ. TRACE. COPY.

on   on

street   street

TRACE. READ. COPY.

on Reed Street

on Main Street

Lesson E Writing

Trace. Read. Write.

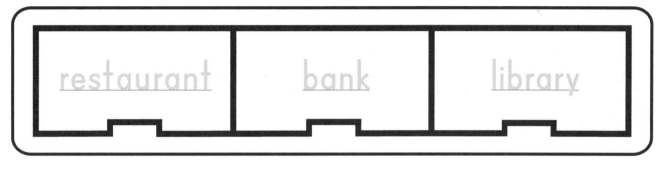

restaurant | bank | library

Reed Street

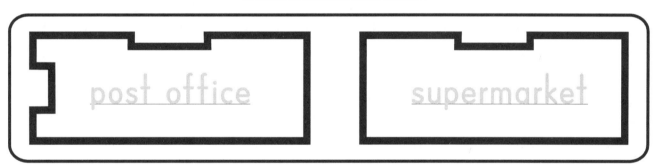

post office | supermarket

The library is next to the _____bank_____.

The _____ is across from the post office.

The _____ is next to the post office.

The bank is between the _____ and the _____.

The bank is on _____ _____.

READ. TRACE. COPY.

school

restaurant

library

hospital

post office

Lesson F Another view

Read. Trace. Copy.

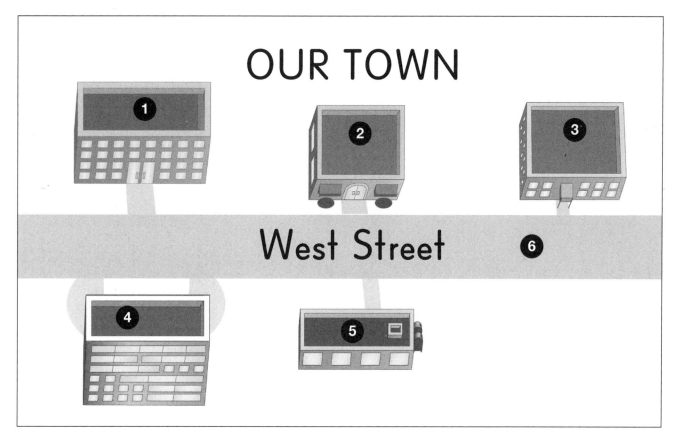

OUR TOWN

West Street

1. school

2. restaurant

3. library

4. hospital

5. post office

6. street

UNIT 6 TIME

Read. Circle the same. 10:00 (10:00) 7:00 11:00 1:00

10:00	10:00	7:00	11:00	1:00
9:00	3:00	8:30	9:00	8:00
6:30	8:30	9:00	9:30	6:30
10:30	1:30	3:10	3:30	10:30

Read. Trace. Copy.

9:00   9:00 _____

10:00   10:00 _____

2:30   2:30 _____

6:30   6:30 _____

Write the time.

_____

Lesson A Listening

🔊 Track 9

Listen. Trace. Copy.

9:00　9:00

7:00　7:00

10:30　10:30

6:30　6:30

Write the time.

7:00

Look. Trace.

C c   C c   V v   V v

Read. Circle C **and** c. Ⓒ ⓒ   **Underline** V **and** v. V v

CLASS   class   MOVIE   movie

Read. Circle the same.   CLASS   class   class   CLASS

CLASS	class	class	CLASS
class	CLASS	CLASS	class
MOVIE	movie	movie	MOVIE
movie	MOVIE	movie	movie

Read. Trace. Copy.

CLASS   CLASS

class   class

MOVIE   MOVIE

movie   movie

Lesson B Events

Read. Circle v.

m o v i e

Write v. Read.

m o __ i e

Trace. Read.

class   movie   TV show

Write.

class _____

_____

_____

Read. Circle the same. class (class) lass (class) lass

class	class	lass	class	lass
is	it	is	is	it
your	your	you	your	you
at	at	as	as	at

Read. Trace. Copy.

Is your class at 11:00?

Is your class at 11:00?

_____

Yes, it is.

Yes, it is.

_____

No, it isn't.

No, it isn't.

_____

Lesson C Is your class at 11:00?

Read. Circle Yes. Yes   **Underline** No. No

Is your class at 12:00?
Yes, it is.

Is your movie at 8:00?
No, it isn't.

Read. Write it is **or** it isn't.

Is your party at 7:30?
No, ___it isn't___.

Is your meeting at 11:00?
Yes, _____.

Is your class at 2:30?
No, _____.

Trace. Copy.

Yes, it is.

No, it isn't.

Look. Trace.

M m M m   N n   N n

Read. Circle M and m. (M) (m) **Underline N and n.** N n

MORNING   morning

Read. Circle the same. MORNING   morning   (MORNING)

MORNING   morning   MORNING

morning   morning   MORNING

Read. Trace.

MORNING   MORNING MORNING

morning   morning   morning

Read. Copy.

MORNING _____

morning _____

Lesson D Reading

Read. Circle m. (m)

m o r n i n g

Write m. Read.

___ o r n i n g

Read. Circle n. (n)

e v e n i n g

Write n. Read.

e v e ___ i ___ g

Trace. Read.

8:00 a.m.   in the morning

8:00 p.m.   in the evening

Read. Write.

10:00 a.m.   in the morning

10:00 p.m.   in the evening

6:30 a.m.   _____

6:30 p.m.   _____

9:30 p.m.   _____

9:30 a.m.   _____

Read. Circle the same. a.m. am (a.m.) m.a. (a.m.)

a.m.   am   a.m.   m.a.   a.m.

p.m.   pm   p.m.   p.m.   m.p.

Read. Trace. Copy.

8:00 a.m.   8:00 a.m.

8:00 p.m.   8:00 p.m.

1:00 a.m.   1:00 a.m.

1:00 p.m.   1:00 p.m.

Read. Copy.

at 11:30 a.m.

at 7:30 p.m.

at 8:30 a.m.

at 6:00 a.m.

at 12:30 p.m.

Lesson E Writing

Read. Trace. Write.

KIM'S TO-DO LIST

8:00 a.m.   class

10:30 a.m.   appointment

2:00 p.m.   meeting

6:30 p.m.   party

8:00 p.m.   movie

Kim's ____class____ is at 8:00 _a.m._

Kim's _____ is at 10:30 ____

Kim's _____ is at 2:00 ____

Kim's _____ is at 6:30 ____

Kim's _____ is at 8:00 ____

Circle a.m.   (a.m.)   **Underline** p.m.   p.m.

MORNING   AFTERNOON

8:00 a.m. class   1:30 p.m. meeting

9:00 a.m. class   3:00 p.m. appointment

10:00 a.m. meeting   5:00 p.m. party

Read. Trace. Write.

APPOINTMENT   Time: 3:00
3:00 p.m.   in the afternoon

MEETING   Time: _____
10:00 a.m.   in the _____

PARTY   Time: _____
5:00 p.m.   in the _____

Read. Circle. Copy.

JACKSON STREET
ADULT SCHOOL
PARTY!

Thursday, July 12

2:00 p.m.

Room 221

555-7018

The party is in the morning.

The party is in the afternoon.

The party is in the afternoon.

The party is at 2:00 p.m.

The party is at 12:00 p.m.

The party is on Tuesday.

The party is on Thursday.

UNIT 7 SHOPPING

Look. Trace.

S s   S s   O o   O o

Read. Circle S **and** s. S s **Underline** O **and** o. O o

SOCKS   socks   SHOES   shoes

Read. Circle the same.   SOCKS   socks   SOCKS   SOCKS

SOCKS   socks   SOCKS   SOCKS

socks   socks   SOCKS   socks

Read. Trace.

SOCKS   SOCKS   SOCKS   SOCKS

socks   socks   socks   socks

SHOES   SHOES   SHOES   SHOES

shoes   shoes   shoes   shoes

Read. Copy.

socks and shoes _____

Read. Circle s. ⓢ

s o c k s

s h o e s

Write s. Read.

__ o c k __

__ h o e __

Listen. Trace.

socks   dress   shirt   shoes

Track 10

Write.

shoes

_____

_____   _____

Look. Trace.

W w W w

Read. Circle W and w. W w

SWEATER   sweater

Read. Circle the same. SWEATER   sweater   SWEATER

SWEATER   sweater   SWEATER

sweater   sweater   SWEATER

Read. Trace.

SWEATER   SWEATER   SWEATER

sweater   sweater   sweater

Read. Copy.

SWEATER   _____

sweater   _____

Lesson B Clothing

Read. Circle w.   **Write w. Read.**

s w e a t e r   s __ e a t e r

Trace. Read.

sweater   skirt   raincoat   blouse

Write.

raincoat

Read. Circle the same.   how (how)   who (how) (how)

how	how	who	how	how
much	munch	much	much	much
is	his	is	is	his
are	are	are	ear	are

Read. Trace. Copy.

How much is the dress?

How much is the dress?

_____

How much are the socks?

How much are the socks?

_____

How much is the sweater?

How much is the sweater?

_____

Lesson C How much are the shoes?

Read. Circle is . (is) **Underline** are. <u>are</u>

How much is the blouse?
$39.99

How much are the socks?
$3.99

Read. Write is **or** are.

How much _____ the shirt?
$39.99

How much _____ the shoes?
$49.99

How much _____ the dress?
$58.00

How much _____ the sweater?
$35.99

Look. Trace.

B b B b   L l L l

Read. Circle B and b. (B) (b)   **Underline L and l.** L l

BLACK   black

BLUE   blue

BLOUSE   blouse

Read. Circle the same.   BLACK (BLACK) black (BLACK) black

BLACK   BLACK black BLACK black

black   BLACK black black   black

Read. Trace.

BLACK   BLACK   BLACK   BLACK

blue   blue   blue   blue

Read. Copy.

BLUE   _____

black   _____

Lesson D Reading

Read. Circle b.

b l a c k

b l u e

Write b. Read.

___ l a c k

___ l u e

Read. Circle l. (l)

b l a c k

b l u e

Write l. Read.

b ___ a c k

b ___ u e

Trace. Read.

black shoes   a black dress

blue socks   a blue blouse

Write.

_____

_____

Read. Circle white. (white) **Underline black.** black

a white blouse

a black skirt

black shoes

white socks

Trace. Read. Copy.

a white blouse

a black skirt

black shoes

white socks

Read. Copy.

a white skirt

a black blouse

black socks

white shoes

Lesson E Writing

Read. Trace. Write.

Shopping List for Tina
- ☑ a blouse
- ☑ a skirt
- ☑ shoes

Shopping List for Jack
- ☑ a shirt
- ☑ a sweater
- ☑ socks

Tina needs a _blouse_____.

Tina needs a _____.

Tina needs _____.

Jack needs a _____.

Jack needs a _____.

Jack needs _____.

Trace. Read.

TOTAL   total

Read. Circle the same.   TOTAL   total   (TOTAL)   (TOTAL)

TOTAL   total   TOTAL   TOTAL

total   TOTAL   total   total

Read. Trace. Copy.

TOTAL   TOTAL _____

total   total _____

Trace. Read.

total	$6.95
total	$17.00
total	$23.99
TOTAL	$18.95
TOTAL	$2.80
TOTAL	$44.00

Lesson F Another view

Trace. Read. Circle TOTAL. (TOTAL)

L-Mart
57 TOWN STREET
BOSTON, MA 02101

blouse   31.99

shoes   42.00

sweater   25.99

TOTAL $99.98

Thank you for shopping at L-Mart.
Have a nice day! ☺

Read. Write.

The blouse is $ 3 1 . 9 9 .

The shoes are $ ___ ___ . ___ ___ .

The sweater is $ ___ ___ . ___ ___ .

The total is $ ___ ___ . ___ ___ .

UNIT 8 WORK

Lesson A Listening

Look. Trace.

E e E e   H h H h

Read. Circle E **and** e. E e   **Underline** H **and** h. H h

MECHANIC   mechanic

Read. Circle the same. MECHANIC mechanic MECHANIC

MECHANIC mechanic MECHANIC

mechanic   mechanic MECHANIC

Read. Trace.

MECHANIC MECHANIC

mechanic mechanic

Read. Copy.

MECHANIC

mechanic

Lesson A Listening

Read. Circle e. (e)

m e c h a n i c

Write e. Read.

m ___ c h a n i c

Read. Circle h. (h)

c a s h i e r

Write h. Read.

c a s ___ i e r

Listen. Trace.

mechanic   cashier   receptionist

◀)) Track 11

Write.

mechanic

Look. Trace.

F f   F   f   T t   T   t

Read. Circle T and t. (T) (t)   **Underline F and f.** F f

COUNT   count   FIX   fix

Read. Circle the same.   COUNT   (COUNT)   count   (COUNT)

COUNT   COUNT   count   COUNT

count   count   COUNT   count

FIX   FIX   fix   FIX

fix   FIX   fix   fix

Read. Trace. Copy.

COUNT   COUNT

count   count

FIX   FIX

fix   fix

Lesson B Job duties

Read. Circle t. t

c o u n t

f i r s t

Write t. Read.

c o u n ___

f i r s ___

Read. Circle f. f

f i x

f i r s t

Write f. Read.

___ i x

___ i r s t

Trace. Read.

counts money   fixes cars   serves food

Write.

_____

_____

Read. Circle the same. yes (yes) year yen

yes	yes	year	yen
no	an	no	on
does	do	dose	does
doesn't	don't	donut	doesn't

Trace. Read.

Does he fix cars?

No, he doesn't.

Does he count money?

Yes, he does.

Lesson C Does he sell clothes?

Read. Circle.

Does she count money?
Yes, she does.
No, she doesn't.

Does he fix cars?
Yes, he does.
No, he doesn't.

Write.

Does she fix cars?

_____.

Does he serve food?

_____.

Look. Trace.

K k K k   U u U u

Read. Circle K and k. Ⓚ Ⓚ   **Underline** U and u. U̲ u̲

TRUCK   truck

Read. Circle the same. TRUCK t̲r̲u̲c̲k̲ (TRUCK) (TRUCK)

TRUCK t̲r̲u̲c̲k̲   TRUCK TRUCK

truck   TRUCK truck   TRUCK

Read. Trace.

TRUCK   TRUCK   TRUCK   TRUCK

truck   truck   truck   truck

Read. Copy.

TRUCK   _____

truck   _____

Lesson D Reading

Read. Circle k. ⓚ

t r u c k

d e s k

Write k. Read.

t r u c ___

d e s ___

Read. Circle u. ⓤ

t r u c k

b u s

Write u. Read.

t r ___ c k

b ___ s

Trace. Read.

bus driver   truck driver

Read. Trace. Write.

What does she do?

She's a _____.

What does she do?

She's a _____.

Read. Circle truck. (truck)   **Underline** bus.   <u>bus</u>

a truck driver

a bus driver

Trace. Read.

a truck driver   a truck driver

a bus driver   a bus driver

Write.

_____

_____

Lesson E Writing

Read. Circle. Copy.

His name is Tim.

His name is Jim.

_____

He is a mechanic.

He is a bus driver.

_____

He drives a bus.

He fixes cars.

_____

Read.

JOB

CASHIER

$12.00 an hour

Saturday and Sunday

ABC Store

Read. Trace. Copy.

cashier   cashier

an hour   an hour

Read. Trace.

$12.00 an hour $12.00 an hour

Read. Copy.

$12.00 an hour

Lesson F Another view

Read. Trace.

HELP WANTED: CASHIER
$12.00 an hour
Saturday and Sunday
ABC Store 555-1289

The job is for a ___cashier___.
The job is $12.00 an ___hour___.
The phone number is _555-1289_.

Read. Write.

JOB: CUSTODIAN
$10.50 an hour
Saturday
6:00 to 3:00
Arbor Library 555-4273

The job is for a _____.
The job is _____.
The phone number is _____.

UNIT 9 DAILY LIVING

Lesson A Listening

Look. Trace.

I i   I i

Read. Circle I and i. Ⓘ ⓘ

WASHING washing DISHES dishes

Read. Circle the same. WASHING (WASHING) washing

WASHING	WASHING	washing
washing	WASHING	washing
DISHES	dishes	DISHES
dishes	DISHES	dishes

Read. Trace. Copy.

DISHES   DISHES

dishes   dishes

WASHING   WASHING

washing   washing

Read. Circle i. (i)

w a s h i n g

d i s h e s

Write i. Read.

w a s h __ n g

d __ s h e s

Listen. Trace.

Track 12

washing the dishes   drying the dishes

making lunch

Write.

_____

_____

_____

Look. Trace.

G g ~~G g~~   A a ~~A a~~

Read. Circle G and g. Ⓖ ⓖ **Underline A and a.** A̲ a̲

GRASS   grass   TRASH   trash

Read. Circle the same.   GRASS ⟨GRASS⟩ grass ⟨GRASS⟩

GRASS   GRASS   grass   GRASS

grass   grass   grass   GRASS

TRASH   TRASH   trash   TRASH

trash   trash   TRASH   trash

Read. Trace. Copy.

GRASS   ~~GRASS~~

grass   ~~grass~~

TRASH   ~~TRASH~~

trash   ~~trash~~

Lesson B Outside chores

Read. Circle g. g

g r a s s

g e t

Write g. Read.

___ r a s s

___ e t

Read. Circle a. a

g r a s s

t r a s h

Write a. Read.

g r ___ s s

t r ___ s h

Trace. Read.

cutting the grass   getting the mail

taking out the trash

Write.

_____

_____

Read. Circle the same. what   who   (what)   hat   (what)

what   who   what   hat   what

doing   doing   ding   doing   do

Read. Trace. Copy.

What is she doing?

Making lunch.

_____

What is he doing?

Making the bed.

_____

Lesson C What are they doing?

Read. Circle Making. Making

What is he doing?
Making lunch.

What is she doing?
Making the bed.

Write.

What is she doing?

_____ .

What is he doing?

_____ .

Look. Trace.

R r R r D d D d

Read. Circle R and r. (R)(r) **Underline D and d.** D̲ d̲

ROOM   room

BEDROOM   bedroom

Read. Circle the same. BEDROOM (BEDROOM) bedroom

BEDROOM BEDROOM bedroom

bedroom   bedroom   BEDROOM

Read. Trace.

BEDROOM BEDROOM BEDROOM

room   room   room

Read. Copy.

ROOM   _____

bedroom   _____

Lesson D Reading

Read. Circle r. (r)

b e d r o o m

b a t h r o o m

Write r. Read.

b e d __ o o m

b a t h __ o o m

Read. Circle d. (d)

b e d r o o m

d i n i n g   r o o m

Write d. Read.

b e __ r o o m

__ i n i n g   r o o m

Trace. Read.

the bedroom   the bathroom   the dining room

Read. Trace. Write.

What room is this?

The _____ .

What room is this?

The _____ .

Read. Trace.

washing   washing   washing

taking out   taking out   taking out

the car   the car   the car

the trash   the trash   the trash

the dishes   the dishes   the dishes

Read. Trace. Copy.

washing the car

washing the car

taking out the trash

taking out the trash

washing the dishes

washing the dishes

Lesson E Writing

Read. Circle.

What is Sam doing?
   Washing the dishes.
   (Washing the car.)

What is Carla doing?
   Taking out the trash.
   Getting the mail.

Read. Write.

What is Sam doing?

_____ .

What is Carla doing?

_____ .

Read.

Chore	Mom	Dad
walk the dog	✓	
water the grass		✓
wash the dishes	✓	
wash the car		✓

Trace. Copy.

Mom: walk the dog _____

_____

wash the dishes _____

_____

Dad: water the grass _____

_____

wash the car _____

_____

Lesson F Another view

Read. Trace. Write.

Home Cleaning Service

Date: April 28

Work Order for: 410 Main Street

Name	Chore
Eva	water the grass
Don	walk the dog
Kay	wash the car

Eva is _watering the grass_ .

Don is _____ .

Kay is _____ .

Lesson A Listening

Look. Trace.

P p P p   AY ay   AY ay

Read. Circle P **and** p. P p **Underline** AY **and** ay. AY ay

PLAY   play

Read. Circle the same.   PLAY PLAY play PLAY PLAY

| PLAY | PLAY | play | PLAY | PLAY |
| play | play | PLAY | play | play |

Read. Trace.

PLAY   PLAY PLAY PLAY PLAY

play   play play play play

Read. Copy.

PLAY   _____

play   _____

Read. Circle ay. (ay)

p l a y

d a y

Write ay. Read.

p l ___ ___

d ___ ___

Listen. Trace.

play basketball   play cards   dance

◀) Track 13

Write.

_____

_____

_____

Look. Trace.

CH ch   CH ch

Read. Circle CH and ch. (CH) (ch)

WATCH   watch

Read. Circle the same.   WATCH   watch   (WATCH)   watch

WATCH   watch   WATCH   watch

watch   watch   WATCH   WATCH

Read. Trace.

WATCH   WATCH   WATCH   WATCH

watch   watch   watch   watch

Read. Copy.

WATCH   _____

watch   _____

Lesson B Around the house

Read. Circle ch.

w a t c h

c h a i r

m u c h

Write ch. Read.

w a t ___ ___

___ ___ a i r

m u ___ ___

Trace. Read.

listen to music watch TV play the guitar

Write.

_____

_____

_____

Read. Circle the same.   like to   (like to)   bike to   lie to

like to	like to	bike to	lie to
likes to	bikes to	likes to	lies to
swim	swim	wins	swims

Read. Trace. Copy.

They like to swim.

They like to swim.

He likes to swim.

He likes to swim.

Lesson C I like to watch TV.

Read. Circle.

What does she like to do?

She likes to play cards.

She likes to swim.

What do they like to do?

They like to watch TV.

They like to listen to music.

Read. Write.

What does she like to do?

She likes to _____.

What do they like to do?

They like to _____.

Look. Trace.

SH sh SH sh

Read. Circle SH and sh. (SH) (sh)

SHOP   shop

FISH   fish

Read. Circle the same. SHOP shop (SHOP) shop

SHOP   shop   SHOP   shop

shop   SHOP   shop   SHOP

Read. Trace.

SHOP   SHOP SHOP SHOP SHOP

fish   fish   fish   fish   fish

Read. Copy.

FISH   _____

shop   _____

Lesson D Reading

Read. Circle sh. sh

s h o p

f i s h

d i s h e s

Write sh. Read.

___ ___ o p

f i ___ ___

d i ___ ___ e s

Trace. Read.

shop   go to the movies   visit friends

Read. Write.

What does she like to do?

She likes to _____.

What does he like to do?

He likes to _____.

What do they like to do?

They like to _____.

Read. Circle the same.   exercise   excise   (exercise)   (exercise)

exercise	excise	exercise	exercise
cook	cook	cork	cook
dance	lance	dance	dance

Read. Trace. Copy.

exercise   exercise

cook   cook

dance   dance

Trace. Read.

She likes to exercise.

He likes to cook.

They like to dance.

He likes to exercise.

They like to cook.

Lesson E Writing

Read. Circle.

What does she like to do?

She likes to exercise.

She likes to cook.

What does he like to do?

He likes to cook.

He likes to swim.

Trace. Read.

exercise   cook   dance   swim

Write.

What does he like to do?

He likes to _____.

What does she like to do?

She likes to _____.

Read.

> # DANCE CLASS
> Learn to dance!
> Saturday, October 3
> 9:00 a.m. to 12:00 p.m.
> $25.00

Read. Trace.

dance   dance   dance   dance   dance

class   class   class   class   class

Read. Copy.

dance class

Trace. Read. Copy.

The dance class is on Saturday.

Lesson F Another view

Read. Trace.

Guitar Class $50.00
Monday, September 1
9:00 a.m. to 12:00 p.m.   Room A

This is for a _____guitar_____ class.

The class is $ _____50.00._____

The class is on _____Monday._____

Read. Write.

Dance Class $75.00
Saturday, April 3
8:00 a.m. to 4:00 p.m.

This is for a _____ class.

The class is $ _____.

The class is on _____.

Welcome unit

0 0 0 0

1 1 1 1

2 2 2 2

3 3 3 3

4 4 4 4

5 5 5 5

6 6 6 6

7 7 7 7

8 8 8 8

9 9 9 9

Unit 1

L   L   L   L   L

T   T   T   T   T

F   F   F   F

O   O   O   O

C   C   C   C

U   U   U   U

I I I I

H H H H

E E E E

J J J J

G G G G

V V V V

Unit 2

A A A A

N N N N

M M M M

S S S S

P P P P

R R R R

D D D D

B B B B

K K K K

Y Y Y Y

W W W W

Unit 3

a   a   a   a

e   e   e   e

r   r   r   r

i   i   i   i

c   c   c   c

u   u   u   u

d   d   d   d

b   b   b   b

h   h   h   h

Unit 4

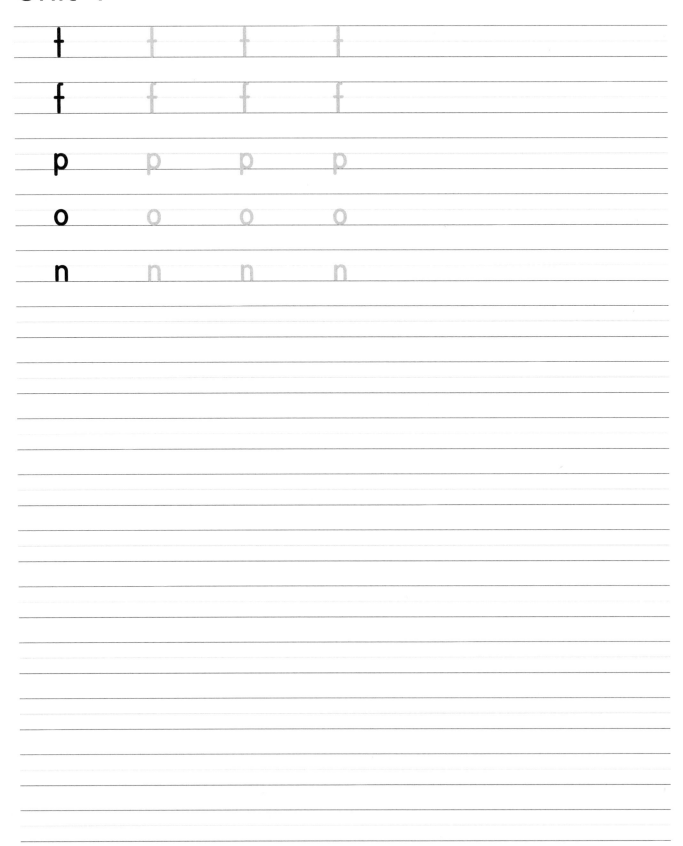

t   t   t   t

f   f   f   f

p   p   p   p

o   o   o   o

n   n   n   n

m   m   m   m

s   s   s   s

l

g   g   g   g

Unit 5

k   k   k   k

w   w   w   w

y   y   y   y

v   v   v   v

j   j   j   j

Unit 6

C   C   C   C

c   c   c   c

V   V   V   V

v   v   v   v

M   M   M   M

m   m   m   m

N   N   N   N

n   n   n   n

Unit 7

S S S S

s s s s

O O O O

o o o o

W W W W

w w w w

B B B B

b b b b

L L L L

I I I I

Unit 8

E E E E

e e e e

H H H H

h h h h

T T T T

t t t t

F F F F

f f f f

K K K K

k k k k

U U U U

u u u u

Unit 9

I I I I

i i i i

G G G G

g g g g

A A A A

a a a a

R R R R

r r r r

D D D D

d d d d

Unit 10

P   P   P   P

p   p   p   p

AY   AY   AY   AY

ay   ay   ay   ay

CH   CH   CH   CH

ch   ch   ch   ch

SH   SH   SH   SH

sh   sh   sh   sh

Additional letters

X X X X

x x x x

Z Z Z Z

z z z z

Q Q Q Q

q q q q

X X X X

x x x x

Z Z Z Z

z z z z

Q Q Q Q

q q q q

Letters and numbers

A B C D E F G

H I J K L M N

O P Q R S T U

V W X Y Z

a b c d e f g

h i j k l m n

o p q r s t u

v w x y z

0 1 2 3 4 5 6

7 8 9

A B C D E F G

H I J K L M N

O P Q R S T U

V W X Y Z

a b c d e f g

h i j k l m n

o p q r s t u

v w x y z

0 1 2 3 4 5 6

7 8 9

ACKNOWLEDGMENTS

The authors and publishers acknowledge the following sources of copyright material and are grateful for the permissions granted. While every effort has been made, it has not always been possible to identify the sources of all the material used, or to trace all copyright holders. If any omissions are brought to our notice, we will be happy to include the appropriate acknowledgements on reprinting and in the next update to the digital edition, as applicable.

Key: TL = Top Left, TC = Top Center, TR = Top Right, BL = Below Left, BC = Below Center, BR = Below Right, C = Center, L = Left, R = Right, CR = Center Right, CL = Center Left, Ex = Exercise.

Photos

All images are sourced from GettyImages.

p. 11 (L): SensorSpot/E+; p. 11 (R): Carlina Teteris/Moment; p. 14 (T, B): Dougal Waters/DigitalVision; p. 16: ajr_images/iStock/Getty Images Plus; p. 17 (T, B): XiXinXing; p. 26 (pen): akova/iStock/Getty Images Plus; p. 26 (book): Gannet77/E+; p. 27 (eraser): Ryan McVay/Photodisc; p. 27: cover photo from Ventures 3e Student's Book; p. 27 (pen): pamela_d_mcadams/iStock/Getty Images Plus; p. 27 (pencil): Pictac/iStock/Getty Images Plus; p. 36: gchutka/iStock/Getty Images Plus; p. 38: eli77/iStock/Getty Images Plus; p. 49 (sore throat): ajijchan/iStock/Getty Images Plus; p. 49 (cold): Tetra Images; p. 49 (headache): laflor/iStock/Getty Images Plus; p. 61 (TL): Mario Gutiérrez/Moment; p. 61 (TC): LeoPatrizi/E+; p. 61 (TR) and p. 61 (car): Car Culture/Car Culture ® Collection; p. 61 (train):mauvd2000/iStock/Getty Images Plus; p. 61 (bus): John Elk/Lonely Planet Images; p. 69 (T): Caiaimage/Sam Edwards/Caiaimage; p. 69 (C): Westend61; p. 69 (B): Wavebreak/iStock/Getty Images Plus; p. 79 (shoes): benimage/E+; p. 79 (socks): Alexlukin/iStock/Getty Images Plus; p. 79 (dress): rolleiflextlr/iStock/Getty Images Plus; p. 79 (shirt): Rothenborg Kyle/Perspectives; p. 81 (raincoat): Photology1971/iStock/Getty Images Plus; p. 81 (blouse): ARSELA/E+; p. 81 (skirt): bonetta/iStock/Getty Images Plus; p. 81 (sweater): demidoffaleks/iStock/Getty Images Plus; p. 83 (blouse): lypnyk2/iStock/Getty Images Plus; p. 83 (socks): Dawid Kowalik/Hemera/Getty Images Plus; p. 83 (shirt): NadyaTs/iStock/Getty Images Plus; p. 83 (heels): subjug/E+; p. 83 (dress): Grape_vein/iStock/Getty Images Plus; p. 83 (sweater): popovaphoto/iStock/Getty Images Plus; p. 85 (socks): deepblue4you/iStock/Getty Images Plus; p. 85 (dress): Lalouetto/iStock/Getty Images Plus; p. 91 (T): didesign021/iStock/Getty Images Plus; p. 91 (C): Hero Images; p. 91 (B): Zero Creatives/Cultura; p. 97 (T): ColorBlind Images/Blend Images; p. 97 (B): kali9/E+; p. 98 (T): skynesher/E+; p. 98 (B): Mike Watson Images/moodboard/Getty Images Plus; p. 107 (photo 1): mediaphotos/iStock/Getty Images Plus; p. 107 (photo 2): Tetra Images; p. 107 (photo 3): Lane Oatey/Blue Jean Images; p. 107 (photo 4): Tetra Images; p. 109 (T): benedek/E+; p. 109 (B): moodboard/Cultura; p. 115 (T): Tim Hall/Cultura; p. 115 (C): Zachary Miller/Image Source; p. 115 (B): nandyphotos/Getty Images; p. 117 (T): monkeybusinessimages/iStock/Getty Images Plus; p. 117 (C): Goxy89/iStock/Getty Images Plus; p.117 (B): Colin Hawkins/Stone; p. 119 (photo 1): Johner Images; p. 119 (photo 2): Comstock Images/Stockbyte; p. 119 (photo 3): gkrphoto/iStock/Getty Images Plus; p. 119 (photo 4): BananaStock/Getty Images Plus; p. 121 (T): Hero Images; p. 121 (C): Hemant Mehta; p. 121 (B): Wavebreakmedia/iStock/Getty Images Plus; p. 123 (photo 1): JGI/Jamie Grill/Blend Images; p. 123 (photo 2): fstop123/E+; p. 123 (photo 3): Johner Images-Berggren Hans/Brand X Pictures; p. 123 (photo 4): Kathrin Ziegler/DigitalVision/Getty Images Plus.

Illustrations

pp. 2–5: Ron Carboni; p. 22, p. 59, p. 66, p. 67, p. 71, p. 103, p. 106 and p. 113: QBS Learning; p. 39, p. 40, p. 41, p. 94 and p. 95: James Yamasaki; p. 53 and p. 111: Frank Montagna; p. 56 and p. 105: James Yamasaki; p. 93 and p. 99: Bill Waitzman; p. 118: Cindy Luu.

Audio produced by CityVox.